MORE CHRISTMAS PROJECTS FOR PLASTIC CANVAS

LEISURE ARTS, INC. • Maumelle, Arkansas

TABLE OF CONTENTS

GENERAL INSTRUCTIONS

WORKING WITH PLASTIC CANVAS

Plastic canvas comes in several mesh sizes. Five, 7 and 10 are available. The projects in this leaflet are worked on **7 mesh**.

Plastic canvas needs no blocking, making it popular with beginners as well as experienced needleworkers. However, tight tension will cause the canvas to curl. In addition, any distortion or mishandling of the canvas **cannot** be blocked out.

No seam allowances are needed because plastic canvas does not ravel. "Pickets" or "nubs" must be carefully trimmed smooth before the finishing process.

If you find it necessary to mark on the canvas, use a waterproof marker with caution since the plastic canvas will not absorb the ink. A pencil may be more satisfactory, but should still be used with caution.

Throughout this leaflet the lines of the canvas will be referred to as threads even though they are not actually "threads" since it is non-woven. To cut plastic canvas pieces accurately, count **threads** (not **holes**). **Fig. 1** shows how to count threads accurately.

Fig. 1

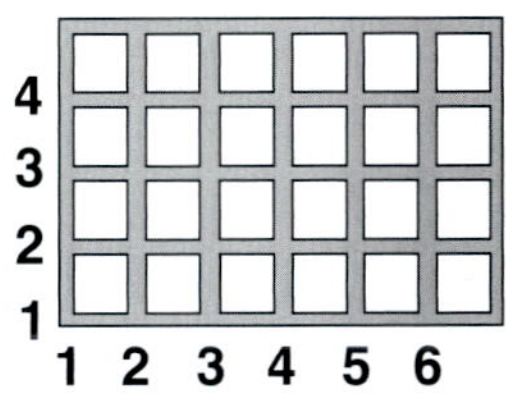

Plastic canvas is washable but acrylic yarn must be used if washing is desired. DO NOT PUT IN CLOTHES DRYER. Plastic canvas **cannot** be professionally dry cleaned. The canvas could dissolve in dry cleaning fluid.

To keep both sides of your work looking neat, it is better to use longer strands to avoid excessive yarn ends since you may not wish to line some projects.

Although any needlepoint stitch may be used, coverage is better with slanted stitches. A double strand of yarn may be needed to insure good coverage on straight stitches.

Worsted weight yarn is used for projects in this leaflet. By experimenting, you may find others satisfactory. Mix different types and sizes of yarn for interesting effects. Use your imagination!

Each of the projects in this leaflet is worked piece by piece. When working each piece, leave 1 thread on all edges unworked. This thread will be covered when joining and finishing. Pieces are joined together using the Overcast Stitch.

Begin Overcast Stitch in the middle of the row where possible. This will make it easier to anchor the yarn and it will also make the corners stronger. It may be necessary to work more than 1 stitch in each hole to ensure good coverage on edges.

STITCH DIAGRAMS

Unless otherwise specified, bring threaded needle up at 1 and all odd numbers and down at 2 and all even numbers. Shaded stitches indicate second row; white stitches indicate fill-in stitches.

TENT STITCH

Fig. 2 shows Tent Stitch method. Any of the three methods may be used unless otherwise stated in individual directions. When working the second row using Continental or Half Cross method, you may find it easier to turn piece upside down.

Fig. 2

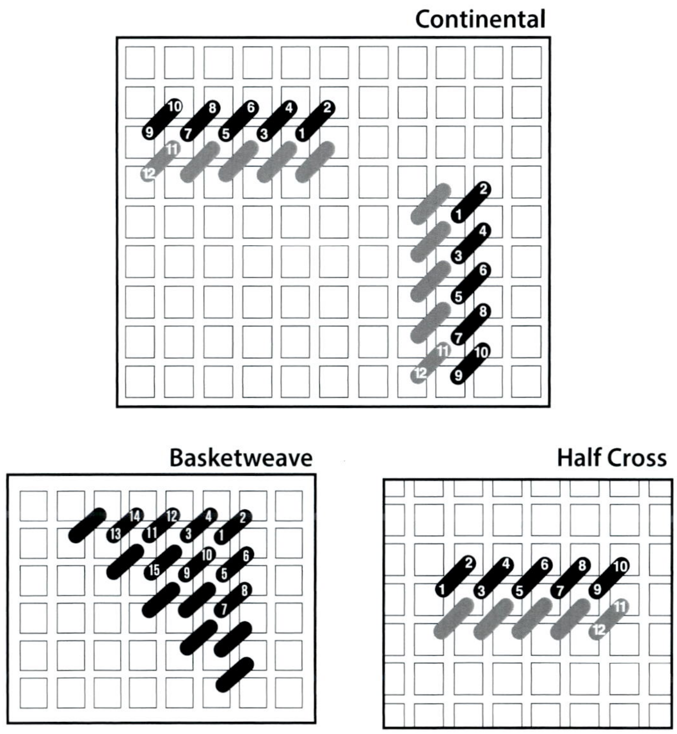

OVERCAST STITCH

This stitch covers the edge of the canvas and is also used in joining two pieces of canvas (***Fig. 3***). It may be necessary to use more yarn to get an even coverage of the edge, especially at the comers.

Fig. 3

SMYRNA CROSS STITCH

This stitch is worked over 2 threads as a decorative stitch to cover canvas. Each stitch ***(Fig. 4)*** is worked completely before going on to the next.

Fig. 4

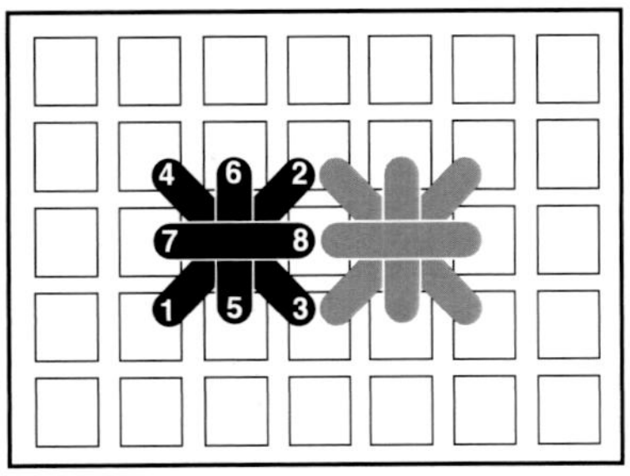

FRENCH KNOT

Bring needle up through hole. Wrap yarn once around needle and insert needle in same hole, holding end of yarn with non-stitching fingers ***(Fig. 5)***. Tighten knot, then pull through canvas holding yarn until it must be released. For a larger knot, use more strands; wrap only once.

Fig. 5

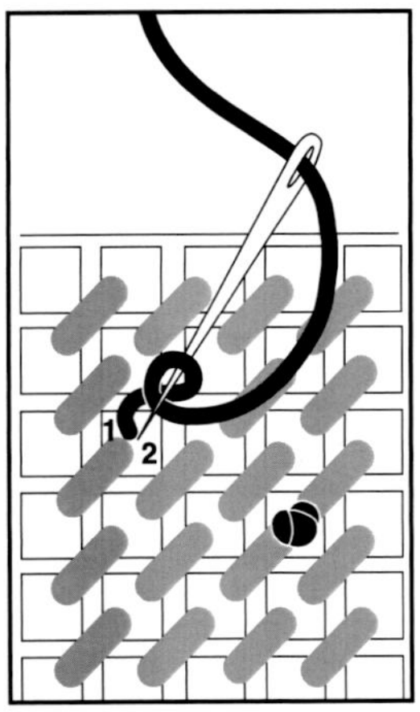

LEVIATHAN STITCH VARIATION

This decorative stitch is formed by first working a Cross Stitch over 4 horizontal and 4 vertical threads. Each arm of the stitch is then crossed systematically as shown in **Fig. 6**.

Fig. 6

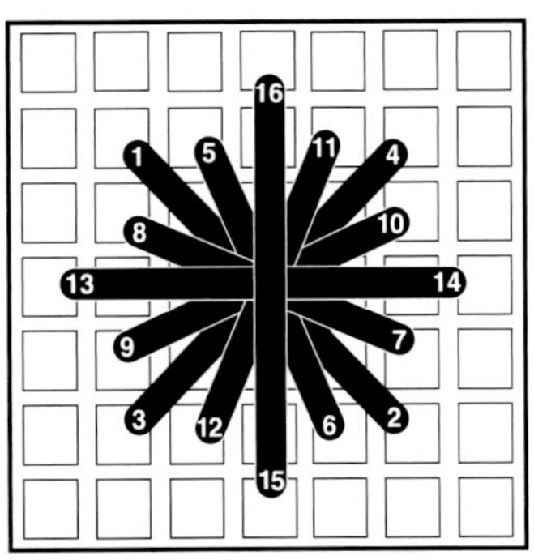

DIAGONAL LEAF STITCH

This decorative stitch combines Gobelin Stitches to create a leaf pattern as shown in **Fig. 7**.

Fig. 7

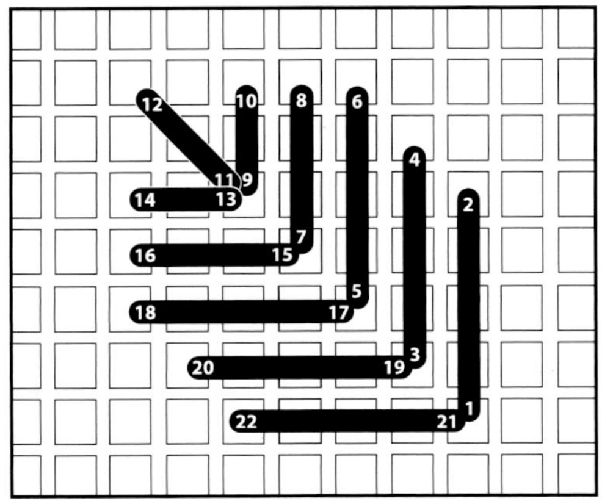

PATTERN STITCH

Gobelin Stitches are repeated in a pattern to create a scalloped effect as shown in **Fig. 8**.

Fig 8

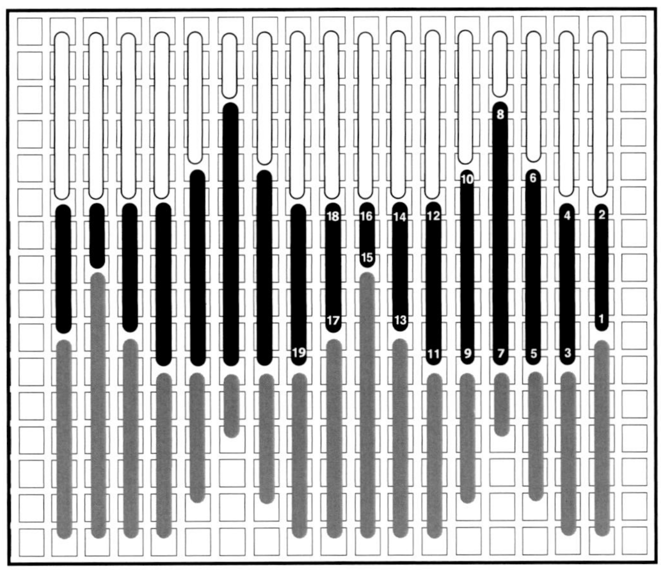

GOBELIN STITCH

This is a basic straight stitch and is worked over a number of threads rather than intersections. Number of threads may vary according to chart. **Fig. 9a** shows the stitch worked vertically and **Fig. 9b** shows the stitch worked horizontally.

Fig 9a

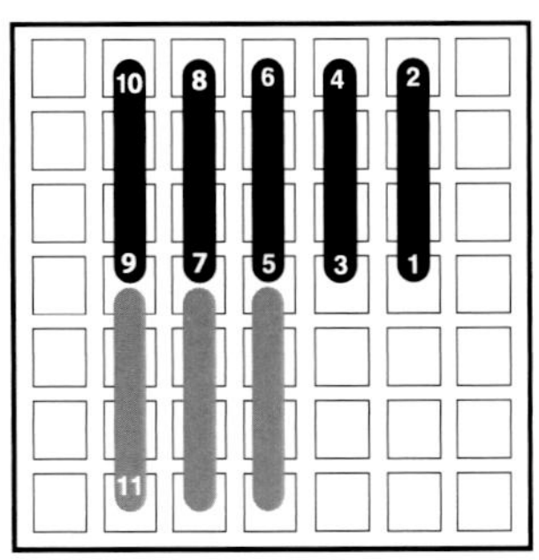

Fig 9b

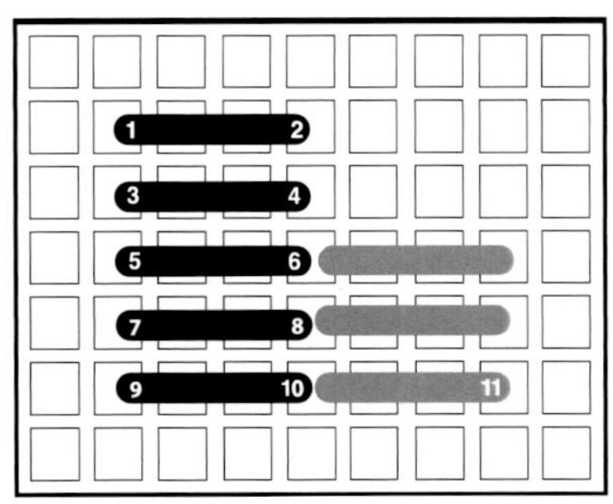

SLANTING GOBELIN STITCH

This stitch covers more than one intersection of threads and may slant in either direction. Number of intersections may vary according to chart. It may be worked either horizontally ***(Fig. 10a)*** or vertically ***(Fig. 10b)***.

Fig. 10a

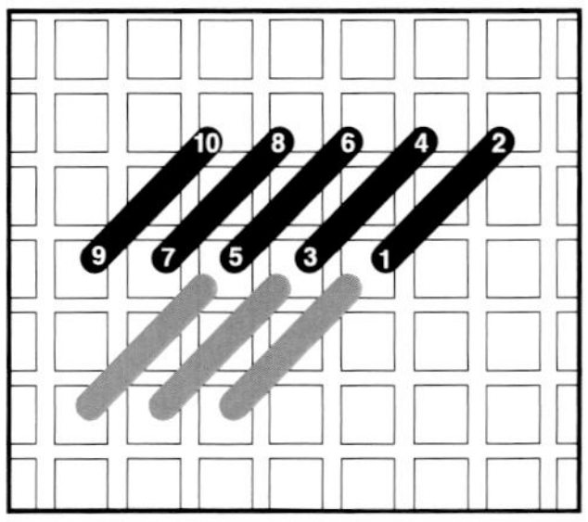

Fig. 10b

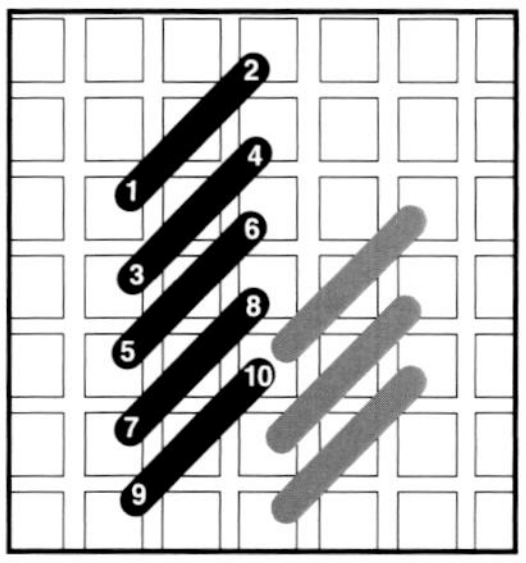

MOSAIC STITCH

The Mosaic Stitch combines three stitches: a Tent Stitch, a Slanting Gobelin Stitch and another Tent Stitch. Complete each unit before starting the next as shown in **Fig. 11**.

Fig. 11

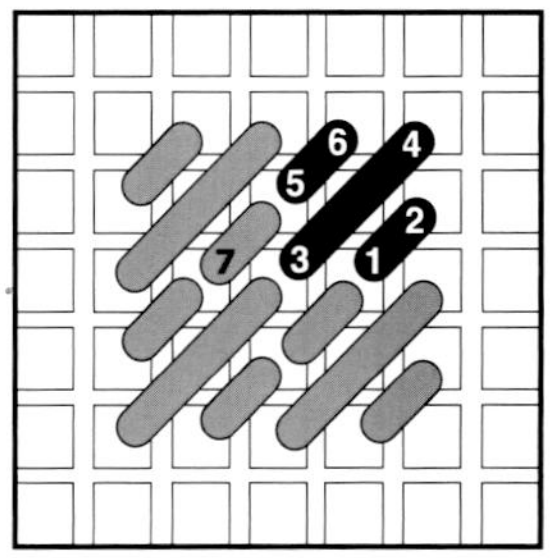

LONG-LEGGED CROSS STITCH VARIATION

This stitch covers the edge of the canvas and is also used in joining two pieces of canvas. Begin by working stitches 1-3. Starting with 4, proceed as shown in **Fig. 12**, forward over 4 threads, back over 2.

Fig. 12

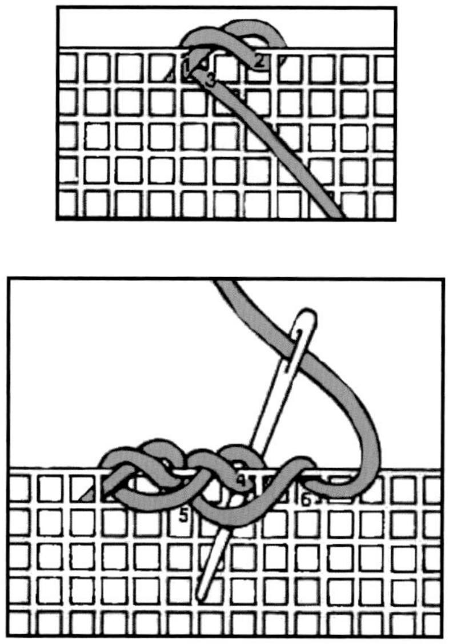

SMALL TISSUE BOX COVER

Shown on Front Cover.

designed by Nancy Dorman; Seaford, DE

SIZE: 4¾" x 4¾" x 5½"

SUPPLIES

7 mesh plastic canvas: 2 sheets, 10½" x 13½" each
Pieces needed:
- Side: 31 x 38 threads, cut 4
- Top: 31 x 31 threads, cut 1
- Long Ribbon: 9 x 35 threads, cut 2
- Short Ribbon: 9 x 25 threads, cut 2

Worsted weight yarn: 50 yds red, 24 yds white and 20 yds green

#16 Tapestry needle

WORKING DIRECTIONS

Side (make 4)**:** Following chart, work Side using Tent Stitch ***(Fig. 2)*** and Slanting Gobelin Stitch ***(Figs. 10a & 10b)***; then work French Knots ***(Fig. 5)*** where indicated.

Top: Cut out opening in Top as indicated on chart. Following chart, work Top. With color of yarn to match stitched area, cover edges of opening using Overcast Stitch ***(Fig. 3)***.

Ribbon: Following chart for Side and leaving one thread on all edges unworked, work holly design on Long and Short Ribbons starting design where indicated on chart. With green, overcast long edges of Long Ribbon. With green, overcast long edges and one short edge of Short Ribbon. Fold Long Ribbon in half to form loop. With white and stitching through all 3 thicknesses, join unworked edges of loop to unworked edges of Short Ribbon as shown in **Fig. 13**.

Fig. 13

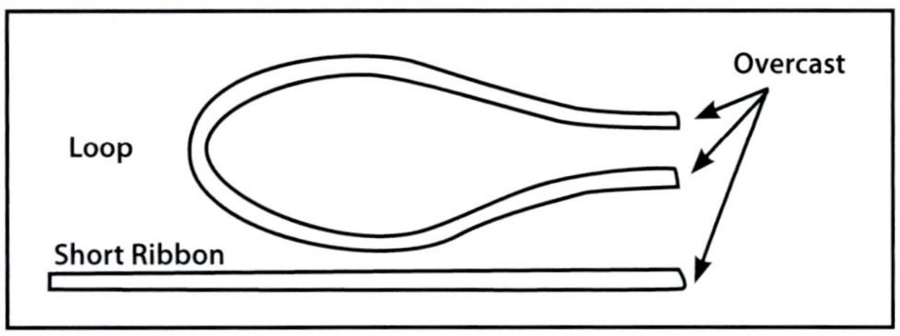

Finishing: With red and matching each long edge, join Sides using Long-legged Cross Stitch Variation ***(Fig. 12)***. With color of yarn to match stitched area, join unworked edge of Top to Sides using Long-legged Cross Stitch Variation. With color of yarn to match stitched area, overcast lower edge. Place ribbons over holly designs on opposite sides of opening in Top and tack securely in place.

Top (make 1)

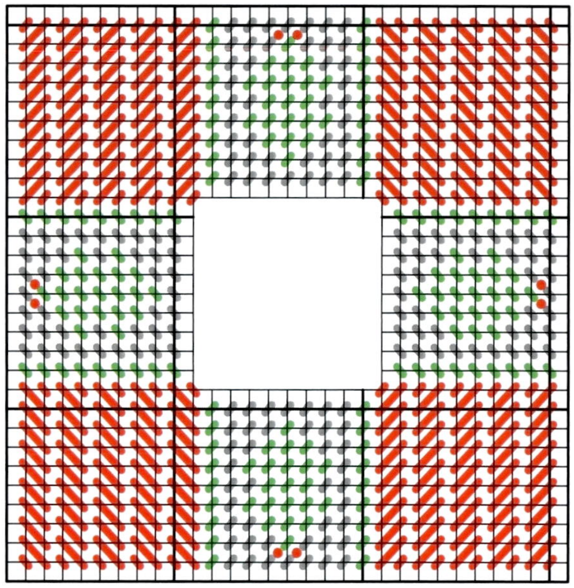

Side (make 4)

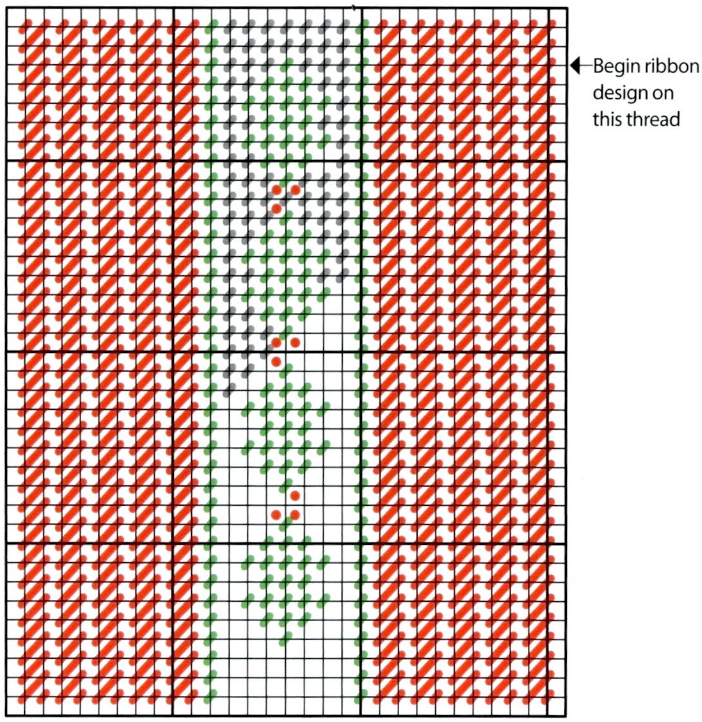

Key
- White
- Red
- Green
- Red French knot

STANDARD TISSUE BOX COVER

Shown on Back Cover.

designed by Nancy Dorman; Seaford, DE

SIZE: 9" x 4¾" x 2½"

SUPPLIES

7 mesh plastic canvas: 2 sheets, 10½" x 13½" each
Pieces needed:
Top: 64 x 33 threads, cut 1
Long Side: 64 x 17 threads, cut 2
Short Side: 33 x 17 threads, cut 2
Worsted weight yarn: 65 yds white, 30 yds green and 10 yds red
#16 Tapestry needle

Note: See Cutting Diagram for cutting layout.

WORKING DIRECTIONS

Special Note: Work Long-legged Cross Stitch Variation for all joining and overcasting.

Long and Short Side (make 2 each)**:** Following charts, work side using Tent Stitch ***(Fig. 2)***; then work French Knots ***(Fig. 5)*** where indicated.

Top: Cut out opening in Top as indicated on chart. Following chart, work Top. With green, cover edges of opening using Long-legged Cross Stitch Variation ***(Fig. 12)***.

Finishing: With white, join Long Sides to Short Sides. With white, join unworked edge of Top to sides. With white, overcast lower edge.

Cutting Diagram

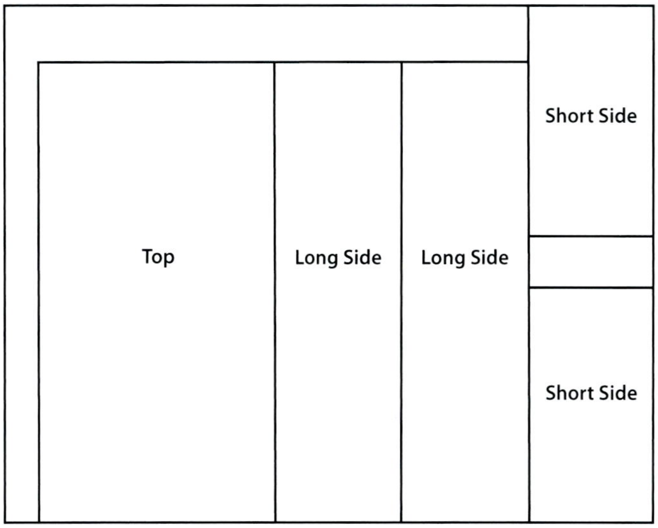

Side (make 2)

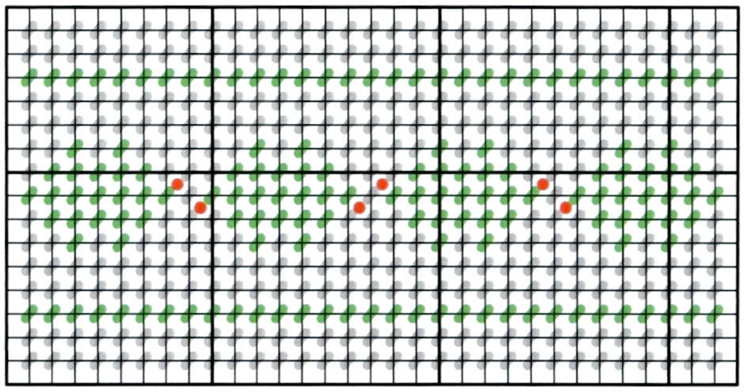

Long Side (make 2)

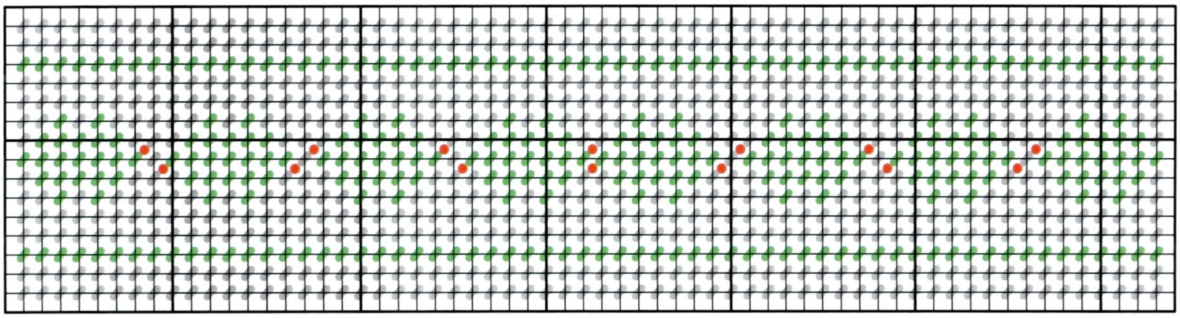

Top (make 1)

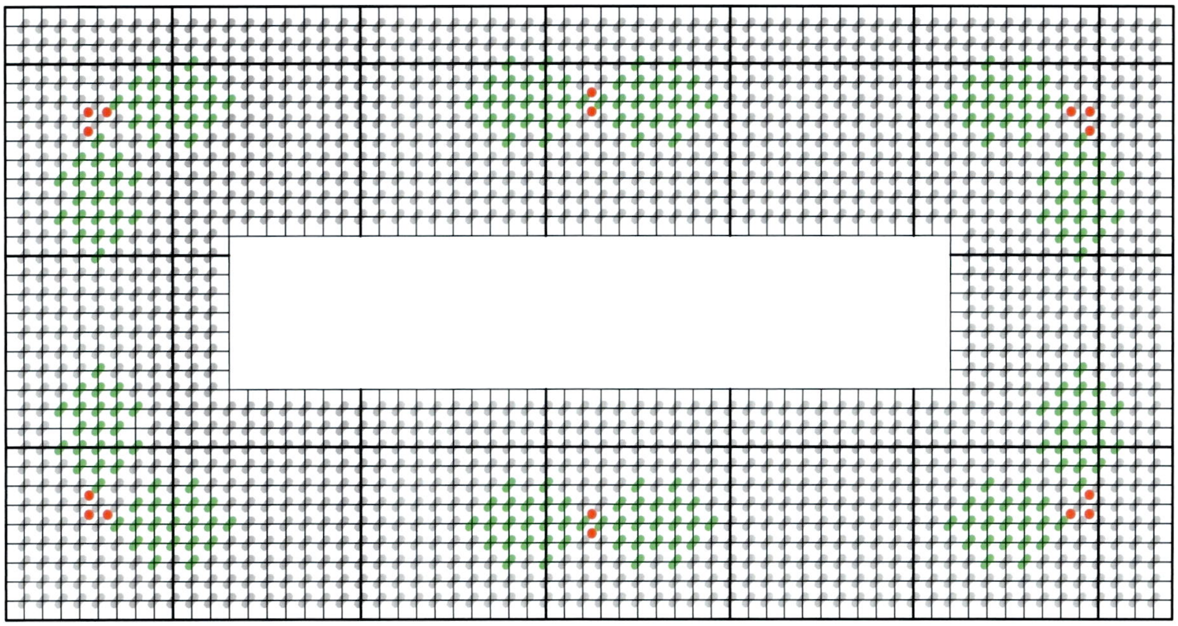

Key

- White
- Green
- French knot

GINGERBREAD HOUSE

Shown on Front Cover.

Designed by Anne Young

SIZE: 7" x 7" x 8"

SUPPLIES

7 mesh plastic canvas: 4 sheets, 10½" x 13½" each
Pieces needed:
Front and Back: Following chart, cut 4
Side: 44 x 31 threads, cut 2
Front and Back Eave: Following chart, cut 2
Side Eave: Following chart, cut 2
Roof Section: 48 x 34 threads, cut 2
Bottom: 44 x 44 threads, cut 1
Worsted weight yarn: 115 yds white, 84 yds tan, 15 yds red, 11 yds green, 10 yds light blue, 6 yds brown, 5 yds each pink and medium blue and 4 yds yellow
Embroidery floss: 1 yd white
½ yd lining fabric, optional
#16 Tapestry needle

Note: See Cutting Diagrams A, B & C for cutting layout.

Cutting Diagram A - Cut 2

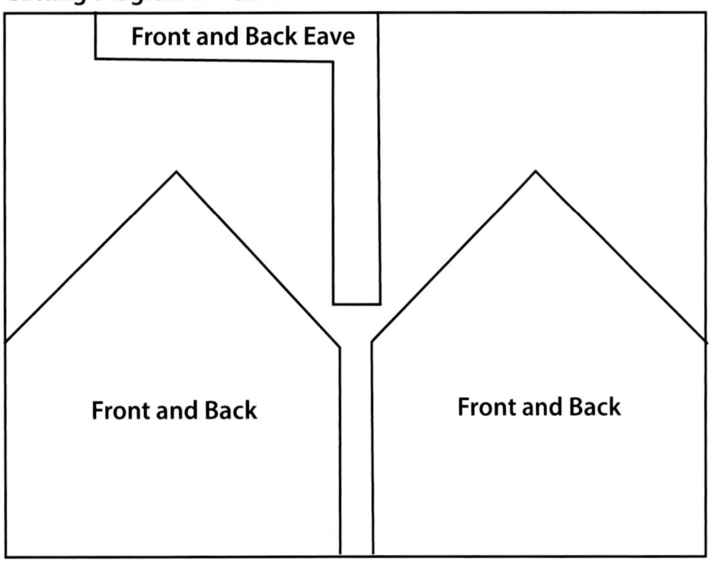

Cutting Diagram B

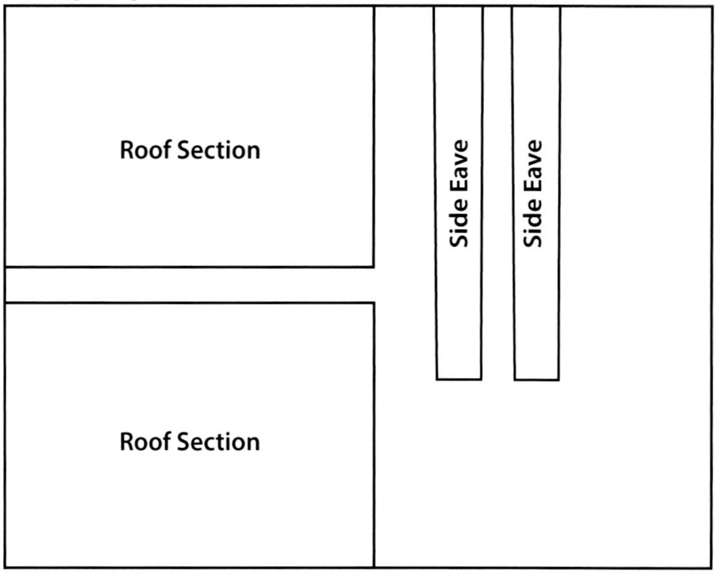

Cutting Diagram C

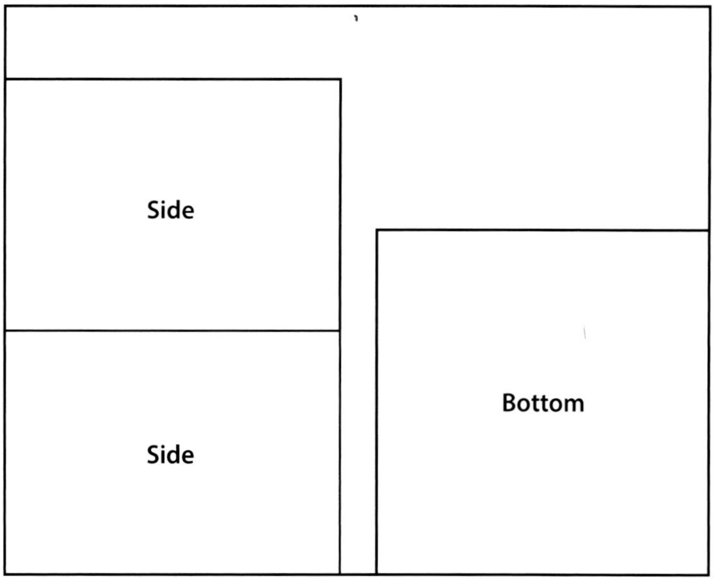

WORKING DIRECTIONS

Special Note: Bottom piece is not stitched.

Front and Back (make 2)**:** ***Note:*** Double piece is used to reinforce Front and Back. Following chart on pg. 10 for shaping detail, trim pieces as shown. Stitching through both pieces of canvas, work Front and Back using Tent Stitch (***Fig. 2***); then work French Knots ***(Fig. 5)*** where indicated.

Side (make 2)**:** Following chart, work Side.

Roof: ***Note:*** Top edge of Roof Sections should be marked for ease in assembly. With double strand white, leaving 1 thread on all edges unworked and starting at long edge, work Roof Sections using Pattern Stitch ***(Fig. 8)***. Following charts, work Front and Back Eaves and Side Eaves using Gobelin Stitch ***(Figs. 9a & 9b)***; then work French Knots where indicated.

Finishing: If you wish to line your house, cut lining fabric for Front and Back, Sides, Bottom and Roof Sections. Do not line eaves. Use your stitched pieces as patterns to cut out fabric; cut lining ¾" larger on all sides than stitched piece. Turn under ¾" on each edge of lining piece and slip stitch to wrong side of stitched piece. With tan and using Overcast Stitch ***(Fig. 3)***, join Front and Back to Sides; then join Bottom. With tan, overcast unworked edges. With white, join top edges of Roof Sections. With white, join Front and Back and Side Eaves to Roof Sections as shown in **Fig. 14**. With white, join short edges of eaves. With white, overcast unworked edges.

Fig. 14

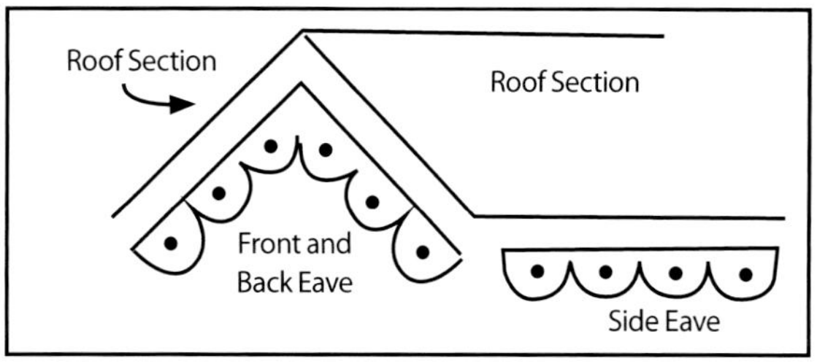

Front and Back Eave (make2)

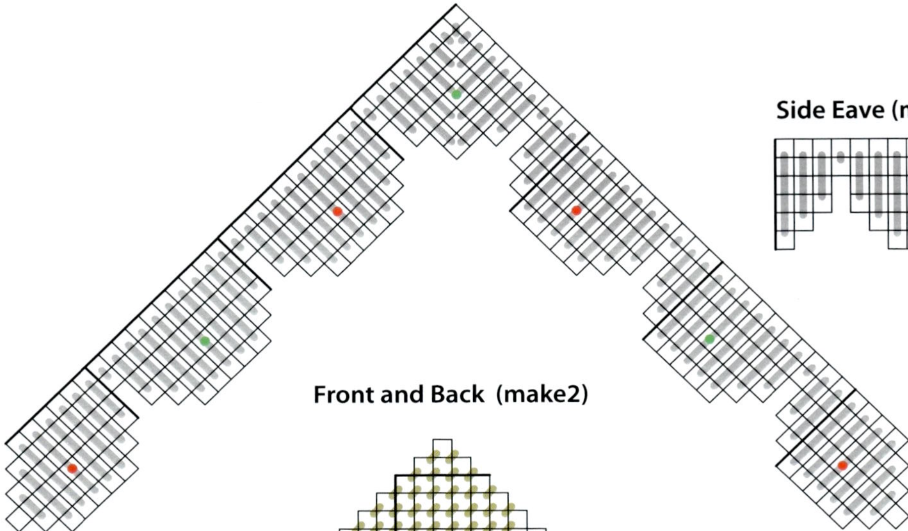

Side Eave (make2)

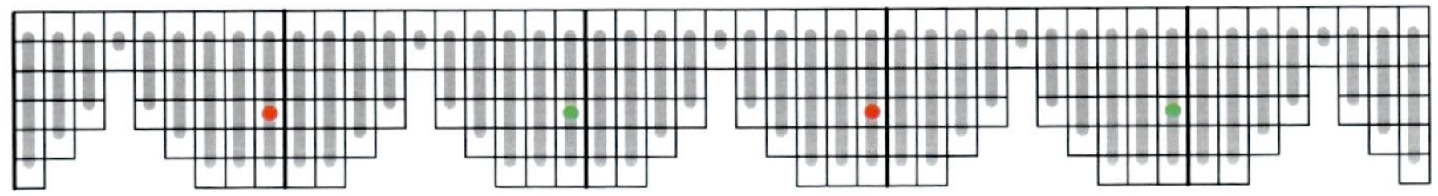

Front and Back (make2)

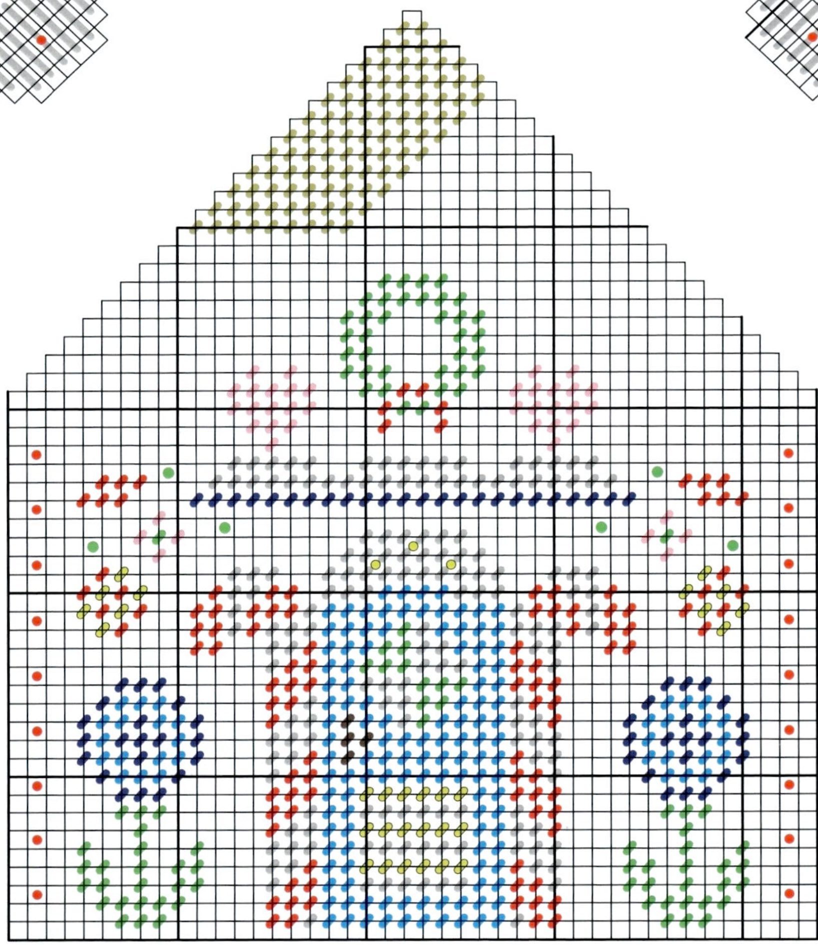

Side (make2)

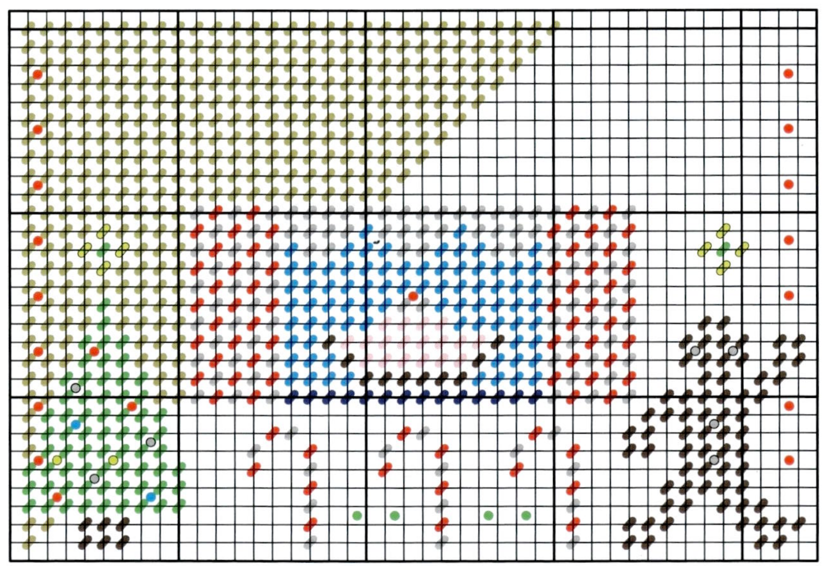

Key

- White
- Yellow
- Pink
- Red
- Lt Blue
- Med Blue
- Green
- Tan
- Brown
- * White French Knot
- Yellow French Knot
- Red French Knot
- Lt Blue French Knot
- Green French Knot

* For Gingerbread Man, use 6 strands of embroidery floss

NOEL BANNER

Shown on Back Cover.

designed by
Julia Penaloza;
North Little Rock, AR

SIZE: 13" x 9"

SUPPLIES

7 mesh plastic canvas: 1 sheet, cut 90 x 60 threads
Worsted weight yarn: 65 yds white, 22 yds red, 12 yds green and 8 yds pink
#16 Tapestry needle
2, 1" white plastic cafe curtain rings
1 yd red $^{5}/_{8}$" grosgrain ribbon, cut in half

WORKING DIRECTIONS

Following chart, work Banner using Tent Stitch ***(Fig. 2)***, Diagonal Leaf Stitch (**Fig. 7**), Mosaic Stitch ***(Fig. 11)*** and Slanting Gobelin Stitch ***(Fig. 10a)***; then work French Knots ***(Fig. 5)*** where indicated. With red and following chart for placement, join cafe curtain rings to top of Banner using Overcast Stitch ***(Fig. 3)*** **and at the same time**, overcast all unworked edges. With sewing thread, attach 1 length ribbon to each cafe curtain ring. Tie loose ends in a bow for hanging.

Key

- White
- Pink
- Red
- Green
- Red French knot

(make 1)

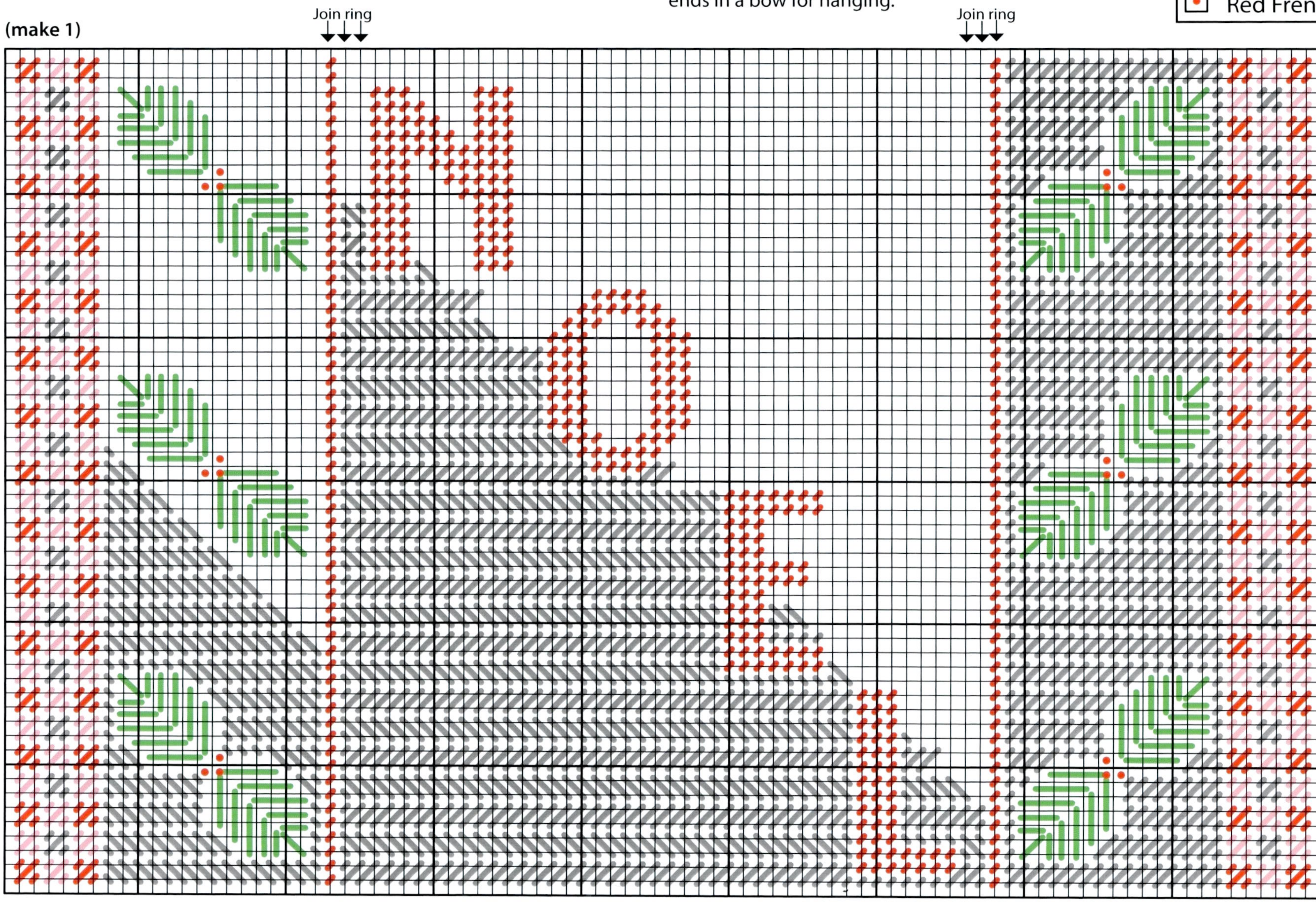

CHRISTMAS TREE PLACEMAT SET

Shown on Front Cover.

designed by Connie Halbrook

PLACEMAT

SIZE: 16" x 12"

SUPPLIES

7 mesh plastic canvas: 1 sheet 12"x 18"; cut 111 threads x 81 threads
Worsted weight yarn: 105 yds red, 20 yds green and 11 yds white
#16 Tapestry needle

WORKING DIRECTIONS

Following chart, work Placemat using Tent Stitch ***(Fig. 2)*** and Slanting Gobelin Stitch ***(Figs. 10a & 10b)***. With green, cover unworked edges using Overcast Stitch ***(Fig. 3)***.

COASTER

SIZE: 4" x 4"

SUPPLIES

7 mesh plastic canvas: cut 27 threads x 27 threads
Worsted weight yarn: 9 yds red, 4 yds green and 3 yds white
#16 Tapestry needle

WORKING DIRECTIONS

Following chart, work Coaster using Tent Stitch ***(Fig. 2)*** and Slanting Gobelin Stitch ***(Figs. 10a & 10b)***. With green, cover unworked edges using Overcast Stitch ***(Fig. 3)***.

NAPKIN RING

SIZE: Approx 2" diameter

SUPPLIES

7 mesh plastic canvas: 7" x 2" piece
Pieces needed:
Napkin Ring: 35 x 9 threads, cut 1
Reinforcement: 3 x 9 threads, cut 1
Worsted weight yarn: 4 yds red, 3 yds green and 2 yds white

WORKING DIRECTIONS

Following chart, work Napkin Ring using Tent Stitch ***(Fig. 2)*** and Slanting Gobelin Stitch ***(Figs. 10a & 10b)***. With sewing thread, baste short ends together to form a circle. Then baste reinforcement over seam on wrong side. With red and working through reinforcement, join short ends together using Overcast Stitch ***(Fig. 3)***. With green, overcast unworked edges.

Key

- White
- Red
- Green

Coaster (make 1)

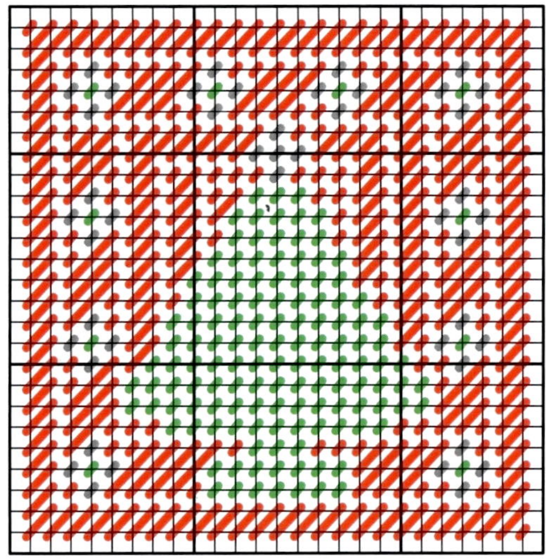

Napkin Ring (make 1)

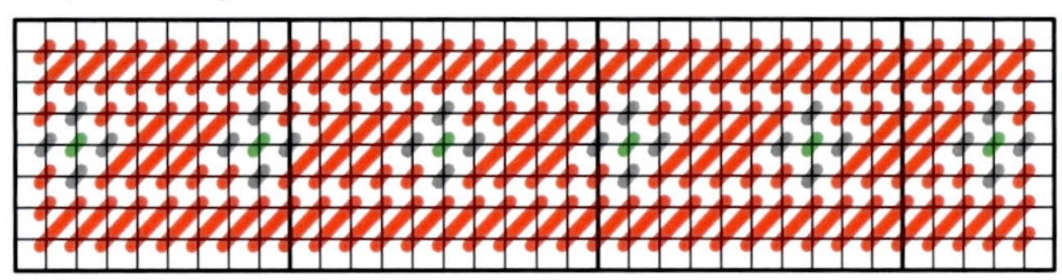

Placemat (make 1)

Candy Cane

Shown on Front Cover.

designed by Nancy Dorman: Seaford, DE

SIZE: 5" high

SUPPLIES

7 mesh plastic canvas: 5" x 6" piece
Pieces needed:
  Front: Following chart, cut 1
  Back: Following chart, cut 1
Worsted weight yarn: 6 yds red and 4 yds white
12" nylon line
#16 Tapestry needle

Key

- White
- Red

WORKING DIRECTIONS

Front: Following chart for shaping detail, trim piece as shown. Following chart, work Front using Tent Stitch ***(Fig. 2)***.

Back: Work same as Front.

Finishing: With red and wrong sides together, join Front to Back using Overcast Stitch ***(Fig. 3)***. Fasten nylon line to ornament where indicated on chart. Knot line tightly 3" from ornament and trim excess end.

Front (make 1)

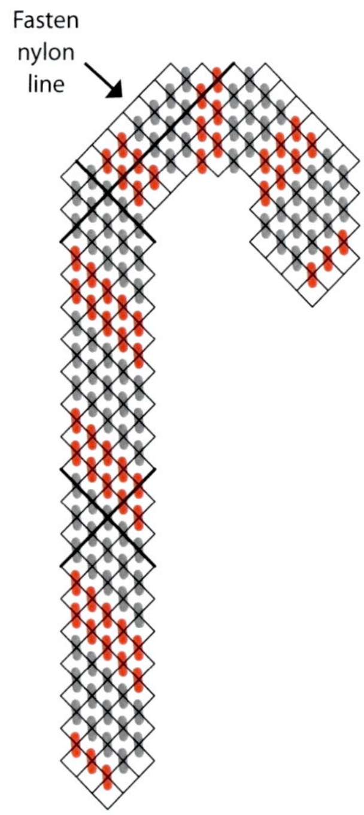

Back (make 1)

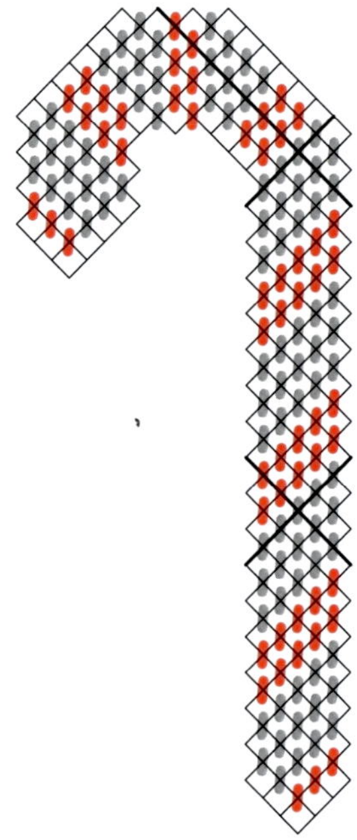

Drum

Shown on Front Cover.

designed by Nancy Dorman: Seaford, DE

SIZE: 2" x 2"

SUPPLIES

3" round specialty canvas: 2 pieces
7 mesh plastic canvas: 2" x 9" piece
Piece needed:
  Side: 38 x 12 threads, cut 1
Worsted weight yarn: 11 yds white, 6 yds green and 2 yds red
1 yd silver metallic cord
12" nylon line
Pipe cleaner
16 Tapestry needle

WORKING DIRECTIONS

Top and Bottom (make 2)**:** Following chart for shaping detail, trim piece as shown. Work following chart.

Side: Following chart, work Side using Tent Stitch ***(Fig. 2)***; then work French Knots ***(Fig. 5)*** where indicated.

Finishing: With white, join short edges of Side to form a circle using Overcast Stitch ***(Fig. 3)***. Fasten silver metallic cord to Side by running needle under stitch directly above French Knot, then under stitch directly below next French Knot as shown in **Fig. 15**. Continue zig-zag design around Side to beginning stitch. Place Top inside circle even with stitched edge. With green and stitching through 2 unworked threads of Side, join Side to Top as shown in **Fig. 16**. ***Note:*** Several stitches may be required in some holes to cover canvas. Cut 2, 2¼" lengths pipe cleaner for drumsticks. Cross drumsticks and tack to Top as shown in **Fig. 15**, Join Bottom same as Top. Fasten nylon line to ornament as indicated on chart. Knot line tightly 3" from ornament and trim excess ends.

Fig. 15

Top and Bottom ((make 2)

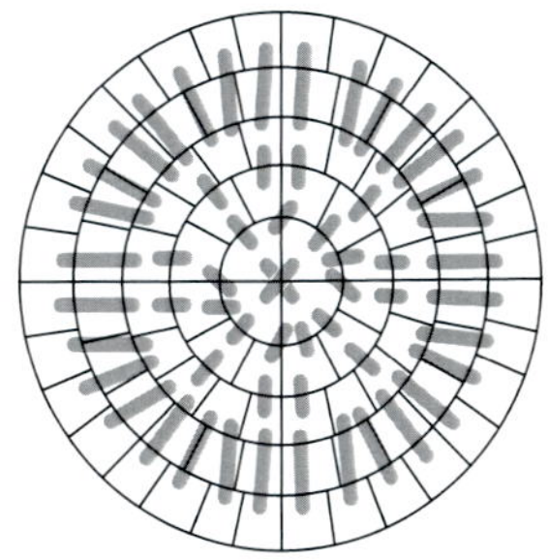

Key
- White
- Red French Knot

Fig. 16

Side (make 1)

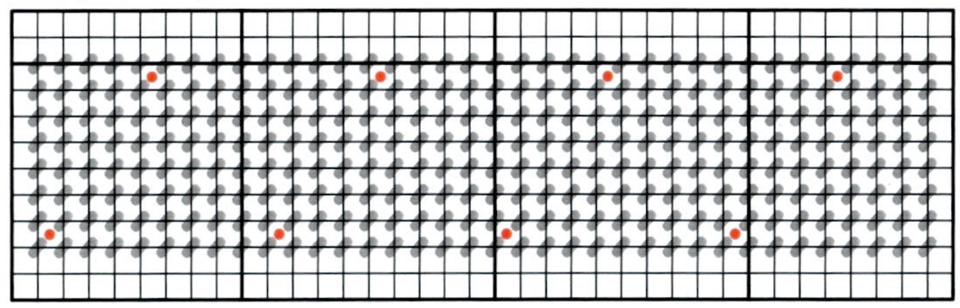

Mouse

Shown on Front Cover.

designed by Anne Young

SIZE: 2½" x 2½"

SUPPLIES

- 7 mesh plastic canvas: 4" x 6" piece
- Pieces needed:
  - Right Side and Left Side: Following charts, cut 2
  - Right Ear and Left Ear - Front and Back: Following charts, cut 4
- Worsted weight yarn: 6 yds white, 2 yds pink and 1 yd each blue and red
- 12" nylon line
- #16 Tapestry needle

WORKING DIRECTIONS

Right Side and Left Side (make 2)**:** Following charts for shaping detail, trim pieces as shown. Following charts, work using Tent Stitch ***(Fig. 2)***; then work French Knot ***(Fig. 5)*** where indicated.

Right Ear and Left Ear - Front and Back (make 2)**:** Following charts for shaping detail, trim pieces as shown. Work using Tent Stitch.

Finishing: With white and wrong sides together, join Right Ear Front to Right Ear Back and Left Ear Front to Left Ear Back using Overcast Stitch ***(Fig. 3)***. With white, attach Right Ear to Right Side and Left Ear to Left Side as shown in **Fig. 17**. With white and wrong sides together, join Right Side to Left Side. Fasten nylon line to ornament where indicated on chart. Knot line tightly 3" from ornament and trim excess ends. With red, tie yarn bow at end of tail where indicated in **Fig. 17**.

Ears (make 1 of each)

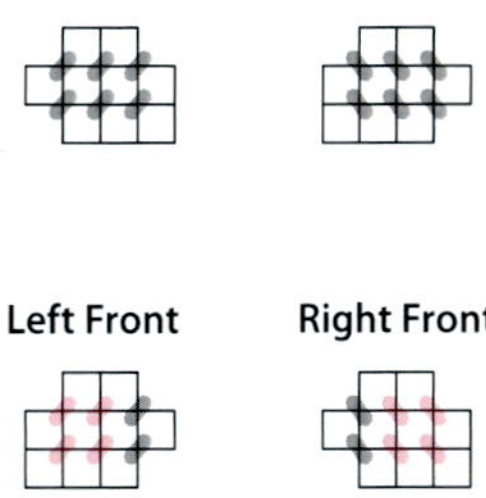

Key
- White
- Pink
- Blue French Knot

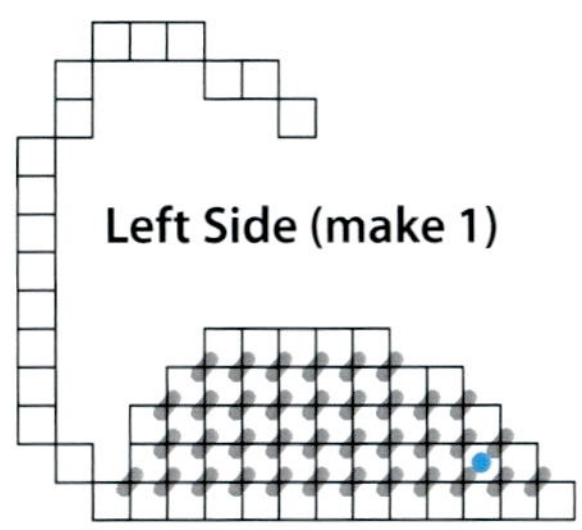

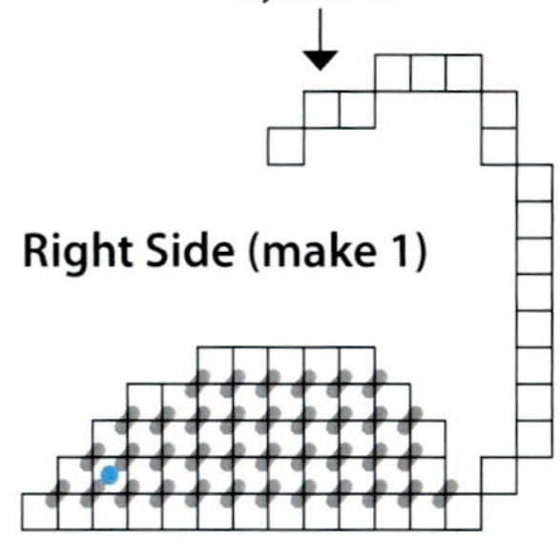

Fig. 17

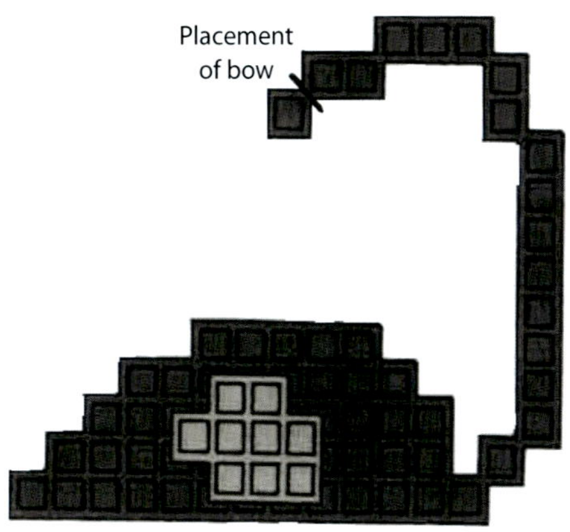

HOLLY DESIGN PLACEMAT SET

Shown on Back Cover.

Designed by Nancy Dorman, Seaford, DE

PLACEMAT

SIZE: 16" x 12"

SUPPLIES

7 mesh plastic canvas: 1 sheet 12" x 18"; cut 113 threads x 83 threads
Worsted weight yarn: 122 yds white, 33 yds green and 7 yds red
#16 Tapestry needle

WORKING DIRECTIONS

Following chart, work border around outer edge using Tent Stitch ***(Fig. 2)***; then work French Knots ***(Fig. 5)*** where indicated. With white and following chart, work center area using Slanted Gobelin Stitch ***(Figs. 10a & 10b)***. With green, cover unworked edges using Overcast Stitch ***(Fig. 3)***.

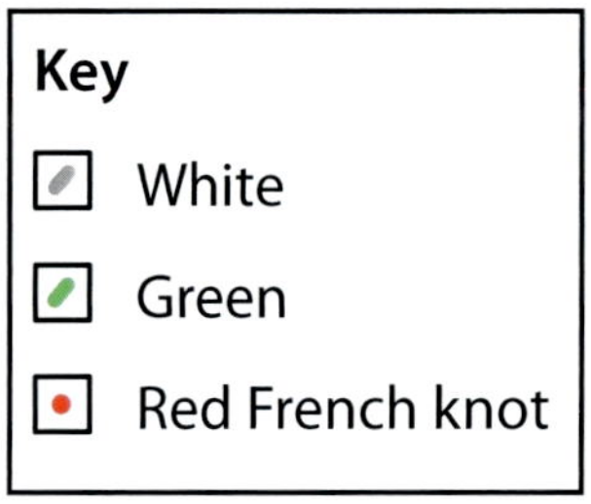

COASTER

SIZE: 4" x 3½"

SUPPLIES

7 mesh plastic canvas: cut 27 x 25 threads
Worsted weight yarn: 8 yds white, 6 yds green and 2 yds red
#16 Tapestry needle

WORKING DIRECTIONS

Following chart, work Coaster using Tent Stitch ***(Fig. 2)***; then work French Knots ***(Fig. 5)*** where indicated. With green, cover unworked edges using Overcast Stitch ***(Fig. 3)***.

Coaster (make 1)

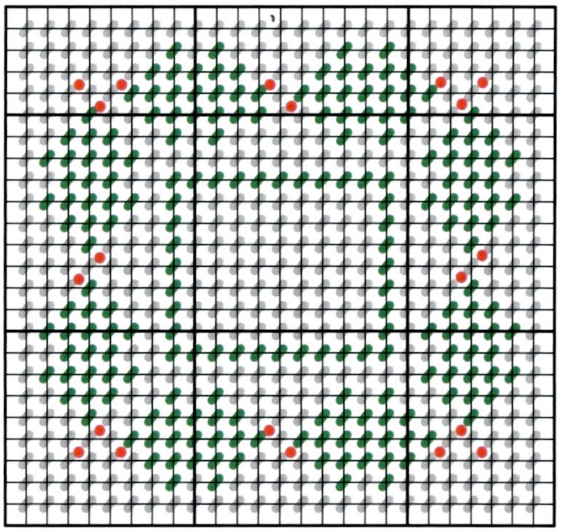

NAPKIN RING

SIZE: Approx 2" diameter

SUPPLIES

7 mesh plastic canvas: 7" x 2" piece
Pieces needed:
Napkin Ring: 33 x 9 threads, cut 1
Reinforcement: 3 x 9 threads, cut 1
Worsted weight yarn: 4 yds white, 3 yds green and 2 yds red

WORKING DIRECTIONS

Following chart, work Napkin Ring using Tent Stitch ***(Fig. 2)***; then work French Knots ***(Fig. 5)*** where indicated. With sewing thread, baste short ends together to form a circle. Then baste reinforcement over seam on wrong side. With white and working through reinforcement, join short ends together using Overcast Stitch ***(Fig. 3)***. With green, overcast unworked edges.

Napkin Ring (make 1)

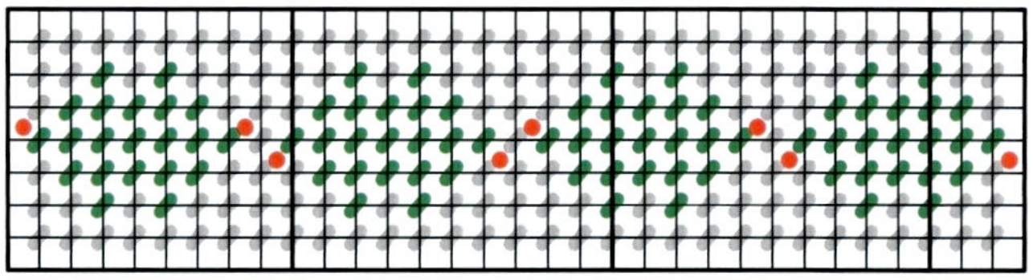

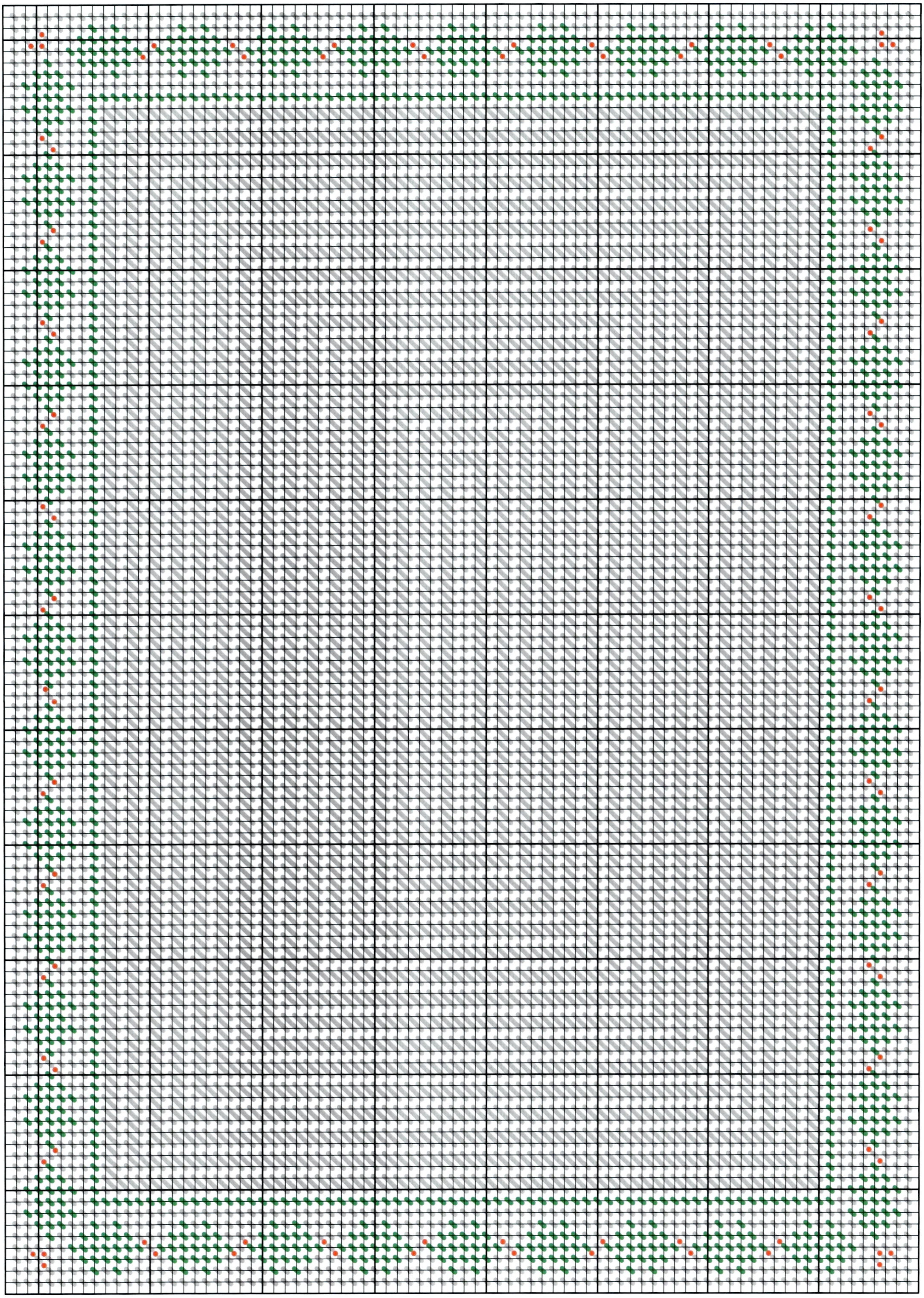

Placemat (make 1)

JACK-IN-THE-BOX

Shown on Front Cover.

designed by Anne Young

SIZE: 2" x 2" x 5"

SUPPLIES

7 mesh plastic canvas: 8" x 11" piece
Pieces needed:
Jack Front and Back: Following chart, cut 2
Side: 12 x 12 threads, cut 4
Top and Bottom: 12 x 12 threads, cut 3
Worsted weight yarn: 9 yds green, 7 yds each aqua and orange, 6 yds yellow and 3 yds pink
Embroidery floss: 12" black and 12" red
12" nylon line
#16 Tapestry needle

WORKING DIRECTIONS

Jack: Front and Back (make 2)**:** Following chart for shaping detail, trim piece as shown. Following chart, work Jack using Tent Stitch ***(Fig. 2)***. With 6 strands black embroidery floss for eyes and 6 strands red embroidery floss for mouth, work features on Jack Front as shown in **Fig. 18**. With color of yarn to match stitch area and wrong sides together, join Front to Back using Overcast Stitch ***(Fig. 3)***.

Fig 18

Box: Side (make 4)**:** Following chart, work Side using Gobelin Stitch ***(Figs. 9a & 9b)***.
Box: Top and Bottom (make 3 — 2 for Top, 1 for Bottom)**:** Following chart, work using Gobelin Stitch. With green and wrong sides together, join 3 unworked edges of Top pieces.

Finishing: With green, join Sides; then join Bottom to form box. With green, join unworked edge of Top to one top edge of box and overcast remaining unworked edges. Center Jack in box. With green, tack in place at top edges. Fasten nylon line to ornament where indicated on chart. Knot line tightly 3" from ornament and trim excess ends.

Key

- Yellow
- pink
- orange
- green
- blue

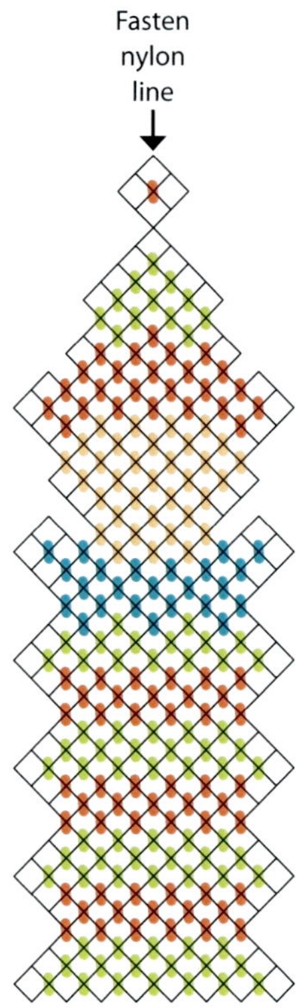

Jack (make 2)

Top and Bottom (make 3)

Side (make 4)

STICK HORSE

Shown on Front Cover

designed by Nancy Dorman; Seaford, DE

SIZE: 2" x 5½", including stick

SUPPLIES

7 mesh plastic canvas: 3" x 4" piece
Pieces needed:
Right Side and Left Side: Following charts, cut 2
Worsted weight yarn: 6 yds each red and white
12" silver metallic cord
12" nylon line
Cocktail straw or pipe cleaner
Small wooden bead (white)
#16 Tapestry needle

Key

Red

White French Knot

Left Side (cut 1)

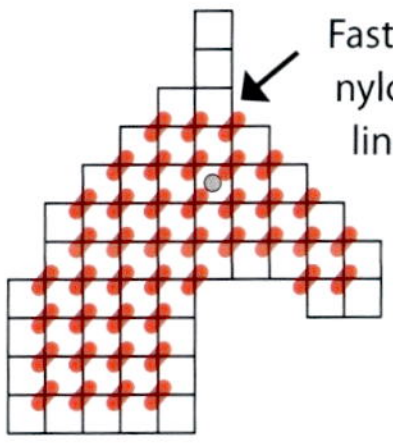

Right Side (cut 1)

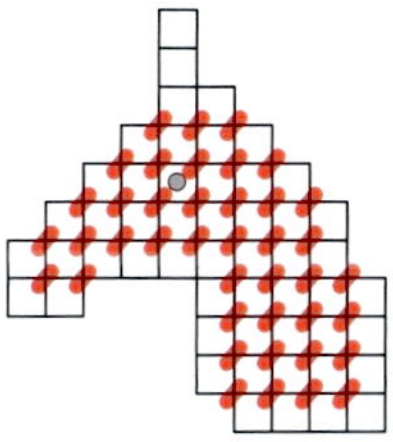

WORKING DIRECTIONS

Right Side and Left Side (make 2)**:** Following charts for shaping detail, trim piece as shown. Work using Tent Stitch ***(Fig. 2)***; then work French Knot ***(Fig. 5)*** where indicated.

Finishing: Glue bead to one end of straw. With red and wrong sides together, join Right Side to Left Side using Overcast Stitch ***(Fig. 3)*** **and at the same time** insert other end of straw between Sides at lower edge. Refer to **Fig. 19** for placement of mane and work as follows. With white, go down in hole (***Fig. 20)***, leaving a ¾" end. Holding end in place with thumb, come up in same hole, leaving a 1" loop ***(Fig. 21)***. Bring loose end and needle through loop ***(Fig. 22)*** and draw strands up tightly. Trim strands ½" from knot. Refer to **Fig. 19** for placement of reins. With 12" silver metallic cord, go down in marked hole, leaving 4" end. Holding end in place with thumb, wrap cord around top of nose and go back through same hole. Knot cord 3" from ornament and trim excess ends. Fasten nylon line to ornament where indicated on chart. Knot line tightly 3" from ornament and trim excess end.

Placement of mane

Placement of reins

Fig. 19

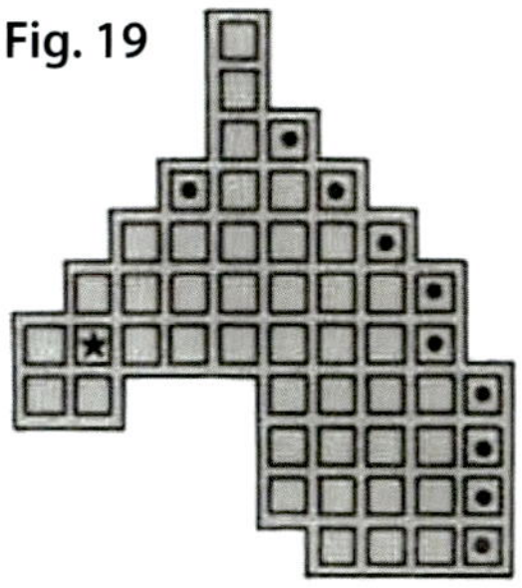

Fig. 20

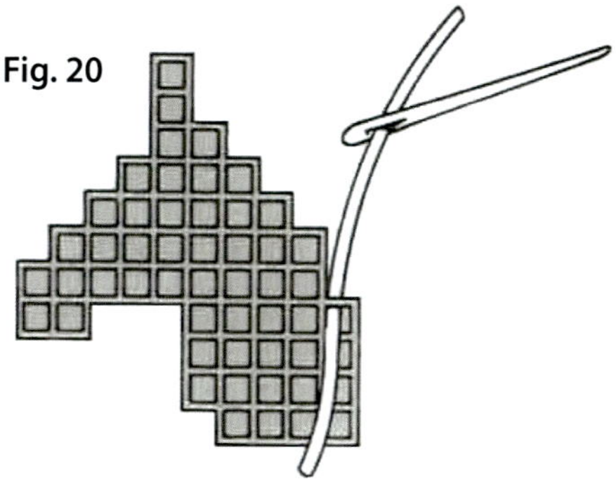

Fig. 21

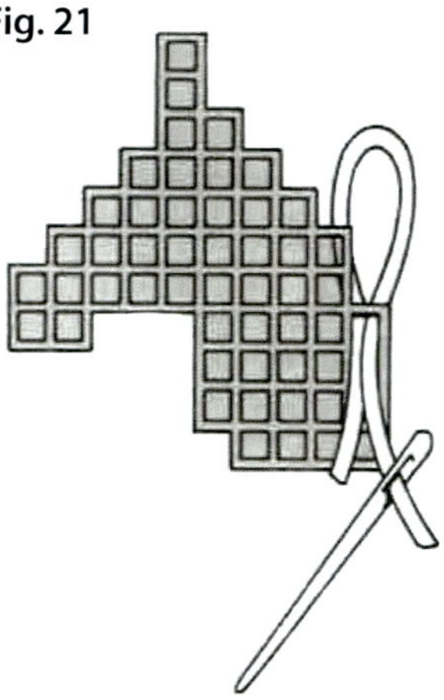

Fig. 22

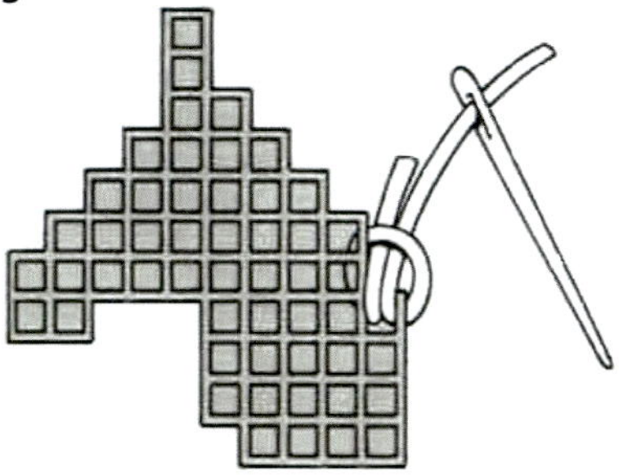

CARD OR NAPKIN CADDY

Shown on Back Cover.

designed by Anne Young

SIZE: 8" x 7" x 4"

SUPPLIES

7 mesh plastic canvas: 3 sheets, $10\frac{1}{2}$" x $13\frac{1}{2}$" each

Pieces needed:

- Front and Back: 51 x 28 threads, cut 2
- Side: 28 x 28 threads, cut 2
- Bottom: 51 x 28 threads, cut 1
- Divider: 49 x 46 threads, cut 2

Worsted weight yarn: 72 yds red, 10 yds each green and white, 7 yds gold and $\frac{1}{2}$ yd brown

#16 Tapestry needle

WORKING DIRECTIONS

Special Note: Bottom piece is not stitched.

Front and Back (make 2)**:** Following chart, work Front and Back using Tent Stitch ***(Fig. 2)***; then work French Knots ***(Fig. 5)*** where indicated.

Side (make 2)**:** Following chart and using double strand, work Side using Gobelin Stitch ***(Fig. 9a)***.

Divider: Following chart for shaping detail, trim curved edges and cut out openings in divider pieces. Following chart and using double strand, work pieces using Gobelin Stitch. With red and wrong sides together, join curved edges of divider pieces using Overcast Stitch ***(Fig. 3)***. Stitching through both pieces, overcast edges of opening.

Finishing: With red, center Divider on 14th lengthwise thread of Bottom and join as shown in **Fig. 23**. With red, join Front and Back to Sides: then join Bottom. Stand Divider upright and tack in place at top of Sides. With red, overcast all unworked edges.

Fig. 23

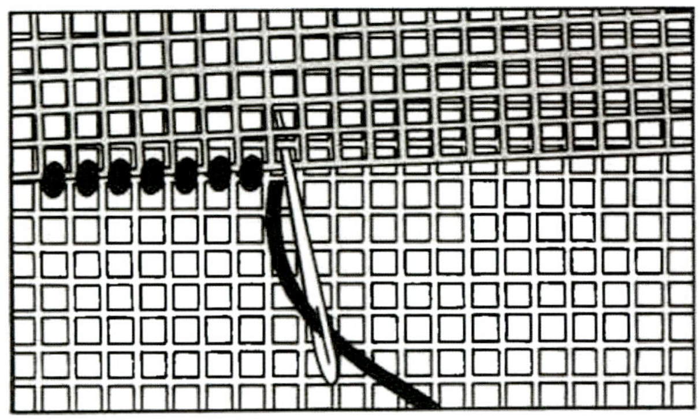

Key

- White
- Yellow
- Red
- Green
- Brown
- Red French knot

Side (make 2)

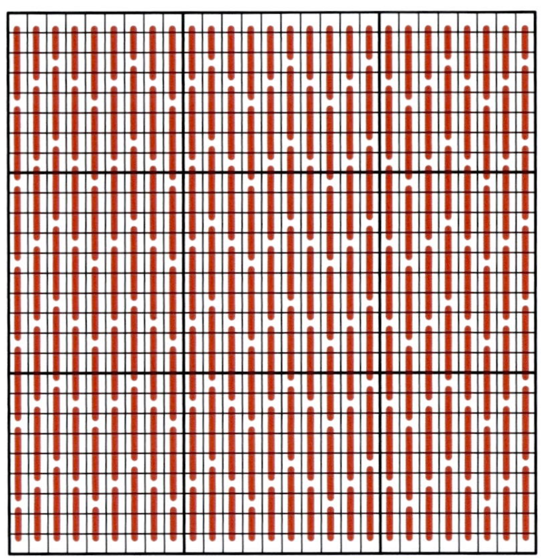

Divider (make 2)

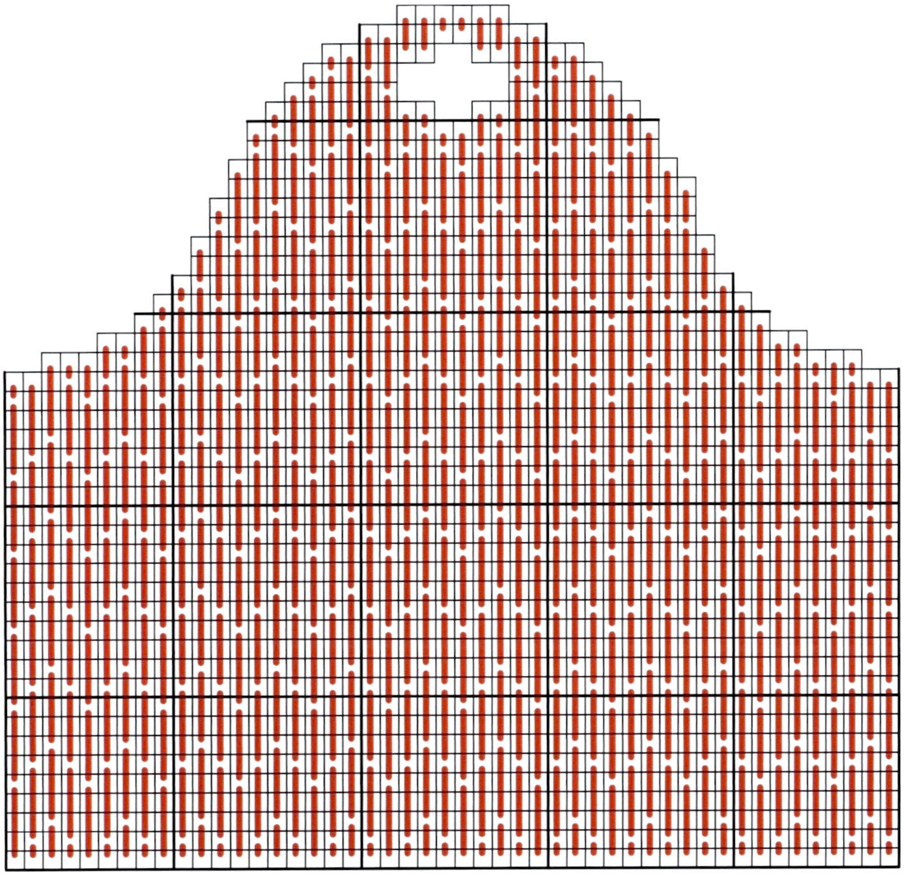

Front and Back (make 2)

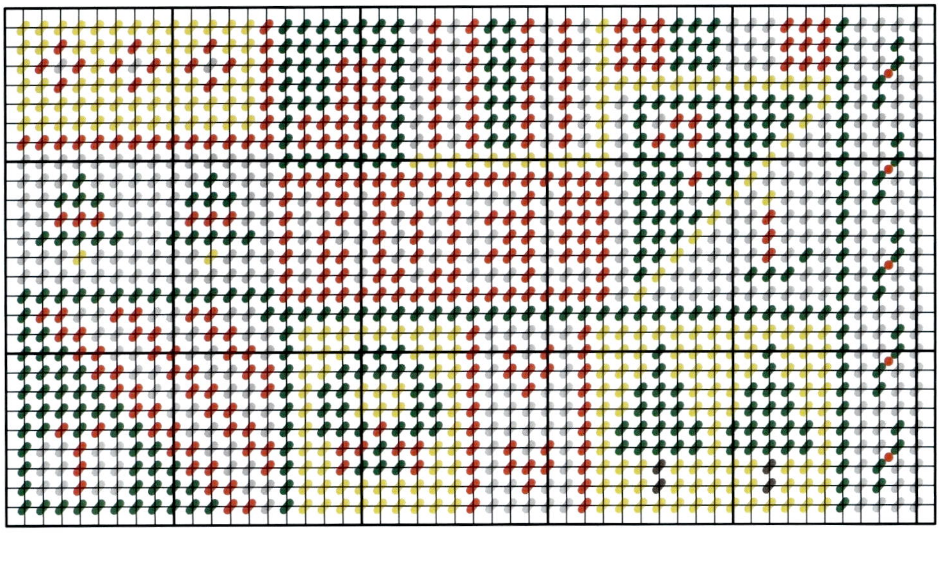

PANDA BEAR

Shown on Front Cover.

designed by Nancy Dorman; Seaford, DE

SIZE: 3" x 3½"

SUPPLIES

7 mesh plastic canvas: 4" x 7" piece
Pieces needed:
  Front: Following chart, cut 1
  Back: Following chart for Front, cut 1
Worsted weight yarn: 10 yds black and 4 yds white
$^{1}/_{2}$ yd $^{1}/_{4}$" red ribbon
12" nylon line
Small amount fiberfill
#16 Tapestry needle

WORKING DIRECTIONS

Front: Following chart for shaping detail, trim piece as shown. Work using Tent Stitch ***(Fig. 2)***.

Back: Following chart for Front for shaping detail, trim piece as shown. With black and leaving one thread on all edges unworked, work Back using Tent Stitch.

Pompom Tail: Cut a strip of cardboard $^{1}/_{2}$" wide and 4" long. Wind black yarn around width of cardboard, 80 to 100 times. Tie tightly in center and cut at opposite side. Trim ends evenly.

Finishing: Attach tail to center Back on 6th thread from lower edge. Tie ribbon in bow and attach bow to Front where indicated on chart.

With black and wrong sides together, join Front to Back using Overcast Stitch ***(Fig. 3)***. ***Note:*** Stuff with fiberfill if desired. Fasten nylon line to ornament where indicated on chart. Knot line tightly 3" from ornament and trim excess ends.

Key
- White
- Black
- Attach bow

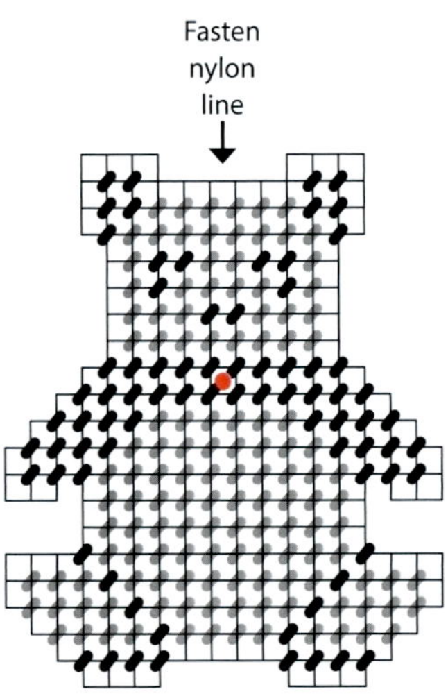

Front (make 1)

WREATH

Shown on Front Cover.

designed by Nancy Dorman: Seaford, DE

SIZE: $3^{1}/_{4}$" diameter

SUPPLIES

$4^{1}/_{4}$" round specialty canvas: 2 pieces
Pieces needed:
  Front and Back: Following chart, cut 2
Worsted weight yarn: 10 yds green and 3 yds red
12" nylon line
#16 Tapestry needle

WORKING DIRECTIONS

Front and Back (make 2)**:** Following chart for shaping detail, trim piece as shown. Work following chart. On Front, work French Knots ***(Fig. 5)*** where indicated.

Finishing: With green and wrong sides together, join Front to Back using Long-legged Cross Stitch Variation ***(Fig. 12)***. With 2, 10" strands red yarn, tie a bow and attach to Wreath where indicated on chart. Fasten nylon line to ornament where indicated on chart. Knot line tightly 3" from ornament and trim excess ends.

Key
- Green
- Red French knot
- Attach bow

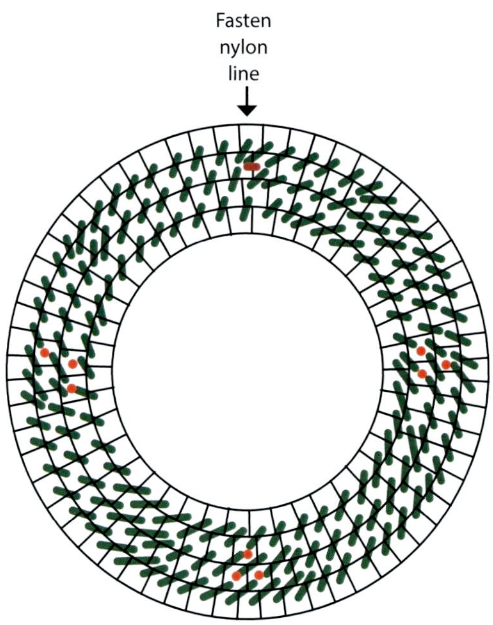

Front and Back (make 2)

STOCKING

Shown on Back Cover.

designed by Pam Speaks

SIZE: 11" x 14"

SUPPLIES

7 mesh plastic canvas: 1 sheet, 10½" x 13½
Pieces needed:
  Stocking: Following chart, cut 1
  Worsted weight yarn: 52 yds white, 14 yds red, 5 yds green, and 5 yds gold
1 yd backing fabric
1" white plastic cafe curtain ring
#16 Tapestry needle

WORKING DIRECTIONS

Following chart for shaping detail, trim piece as shown. Center desired name from alphabet on pg. 24 on marked thread on Stocking and with red, work using Tent Stitch ***(Fig. 2)***.

Following chart, work stocking using Slanting Gobelin Stitch ***(Figs. 10a & 10b)***, Smyrna Cross Stitch ***(Fig. 4)***, Gobelin Stitch ***(Fig. 9a)***, Leviathan Stitch Variation ***(Fig. 6)*** and Tent Stitch. With white, cover unworked edges using Overcast Stitch ***(Fig. 3)***.

Finishing: Use your stitch piece as a pattern to cut backing fabric; cut backing 3/4" larger on sides and bottom and 2" larger on top. Turn under 1/4" on top edge and press; then turn under remaining 1 3/4" and slip stitch. Turn under 3/4" seam allowances on remaining edges, clipping curves where necessary. Slip stitch to wrong side of stitched piece leaving top edge open. Fasten cafe curtain ring to top right edge.

Front (make 1)

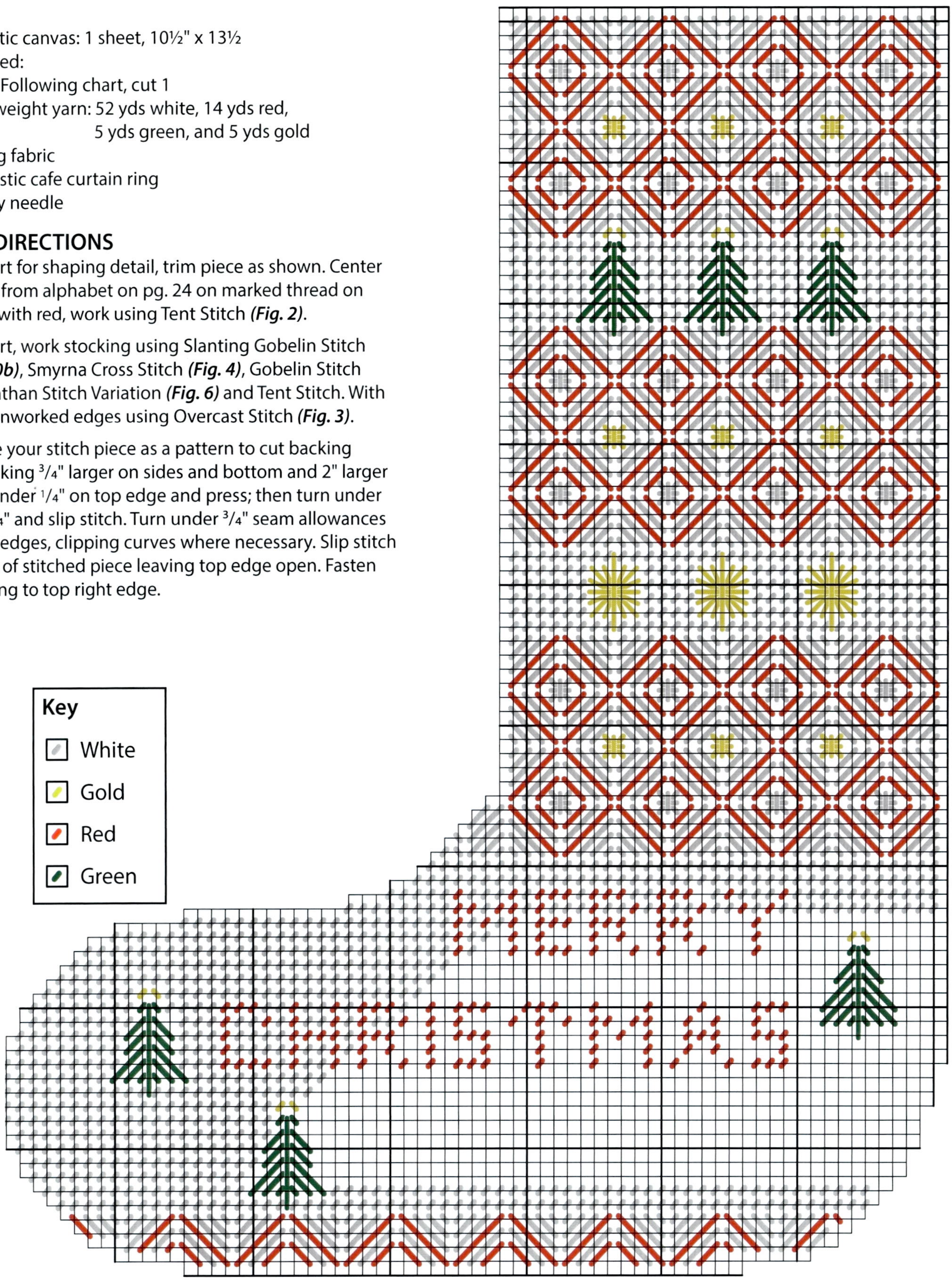

Key

- White
- Gold
- Red
- Green

STAR

Shown on Front Cover.

designed by Anne Young

SIZE: 4" x 4"

SUPPLIES

7 mesh plastic canvas: 5" x 10" piece
Pieces needed:
Front and Back: Following chart, cut 2
Worsted weight yarn: 10 yds red and 6 yds each green and white
12" nylon line
#16 Tapestry needle

WORKING DIRECTIONS

Note: Use double strand throughout.

Front and Back (make 2)**:** Following chart for shaping detail, trim piece as shown. Following chart, work Front and Back using Gobelin Stitch ***(Figs. 9a & 9b)***.

Finishing: With red and wrong sides together, join Front to Back using Overcast Stitch ***(Fig. 3)***. Fasten nylon line to ornament where indicated on chart. Knot line tightly 3" from ornament and trim excess ends.

Key

White

Red

Green

Front and Back (make 2)

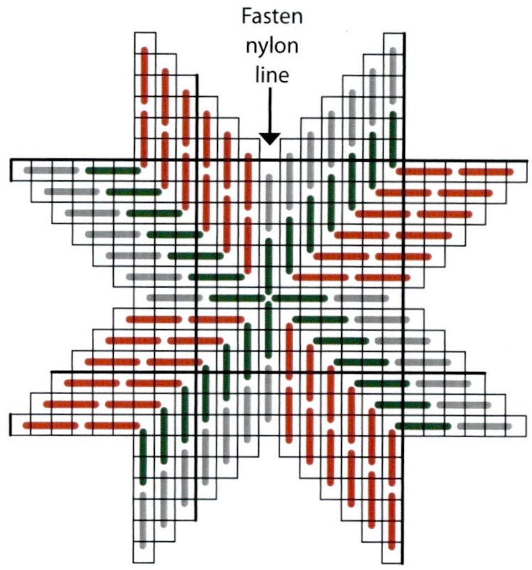

Stocking Alphabet

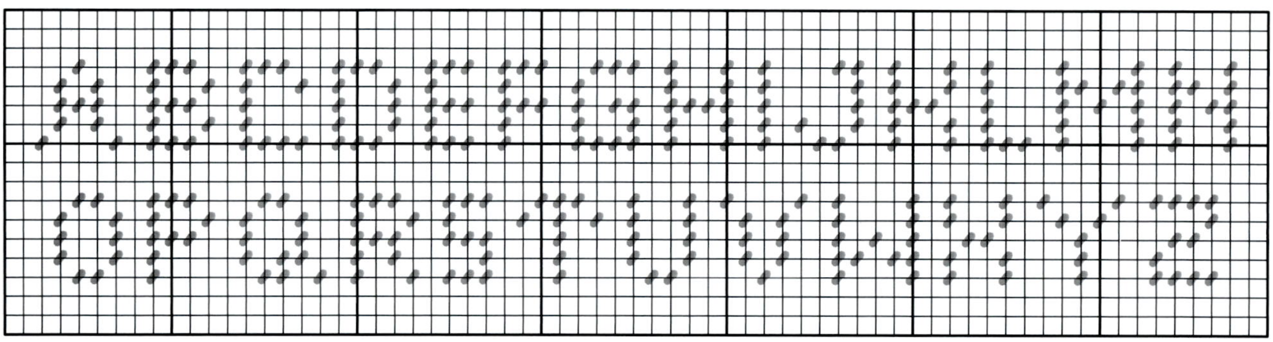

Cover items made and patterns tested by Wanda Baker, Susan Barrs, Beth Collins, Susan James, Carol Lapp, Sara Reinmiller, Christel Shelton and Peggy Tucker.